BRITISH
ISSUES

FUTURE ENERGY

Andrea Smith

FRANKLIN WATTS
LONDON•SYDNEY

First published in 2007 by Franklin Watts
338 Euston Road, London NW1 3BH

Franklin Watts Australia
Level 17/207 Kent Street
Sydney NSW 2000

Editor: Julia Bird
Designer: Thomas Keenes
Picture researcher: Sarah Smithies

Picture credits:
A Room With Views, Alamy: 28; Barry
Batchelor, PA Archive, PA Photos: 10-11; Bosch:
19; Colin McPherson, Corbis: 13; David Hartley,
Rex Features; 18. Edward Parker, Alamy: 29;
Gerry Penny, epa, Corbis: 17; Ian McCarney,
Rex Features; 20. Jason Hawkes, Corbis: 16;
John James, Alamy: 21; Judyth Platt; Ecoscene,
Corbis: 5; Martyn Goddard, GoinGreen, G-Wiz:
24; Paul Glendell, Alamy: 15; Phil Noble,
Reuters, Corbis: 14; Philippe Hays, Rex
Features: 25; Rex Argent, Alamy: 27; Ross
Brown, Stringer, Getty Images: 6; Sally A.
Morgan; Ecoscene; Corbis: 26. Scott Barbour,
Getty Images: 9; The Photolibrary Wales,
Alamy: 22; Wavegen: 17; William Weddle,
Leslie Garland Picture Library, Alamy: 4.

Every attempt has been made to clear
copyright. Should there be any inadvertent
omission please apply to the publisher for
rectification.

A CIP catalogue record for this book
is available from the British Library

ISBN: 978 0 7496 7601 8

Dewey Classification: 333.79'0941

Printed in China

Franklin Watts is a division of
Hachette Children's Books,
an Hachette Livre UK company.

CONTENTS

THE IMPORTANCE OF ENERGY

Energy, in the form of heat or power, is vital to our lives today. From lighting a single lightbulb to heating millions of homes, and from fuelling a single car journey to working with today's vast computer networks, energy is indispensable to virtually every aspect of modern life.

Decision time

Britain's power network, the National Grid, was completed in 1937. Since then, electricity supply to homes and businesses has been more or less assured. Today, people take it for granted that when they flick a switch a light will come on or kettle will heat up, but this may not be the case for much longer. Energy in Britain is at a crossroads, and the decisions we make now will have far-reaching consequences.

▼ An oil drilling platform in the North Sea, off Britain's coast. Oil is a valuable source of energy.

Dwindling reserves

Nearly all power in Britain comes from the burning of fossil fuels – coal, oil or natural gas – either to provide heat directly, or to use heat to generate electricity. For a long time, Britain has been self-sufficient in oil and gas due to reserves under the North Sea. However, our output of gas and oil is now declining and we rely increasingly on supplies from abroad. Added to this, many of our coal-fired and nuclear power stations are reaching the end of their lives. Moreover, it is now widely believed that climate change (see pages 10–11) is caused by the carbon dioxide emissions given off when fossil fuels are burned.

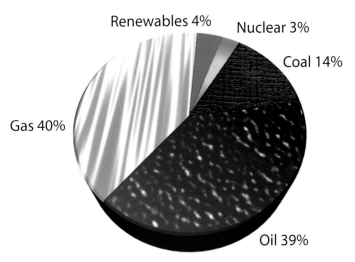

▲ **Sources of Energy in Britain**
A breakdown of the current sources of energy in Britain shows that fossil fuels, especially gas and oil, are still the main providers of energy.

Increasing demand

Over the past 20 years, energy consumption in Britain has increased by one per cent a year. Transport accounts for a large chunk of this increase. Transportation of goods by road, for example, has gone up by 86 per cent in the past 30 years. Air freight has increased by a similar amount, while the number of miles flown by British passengers has quadrupled since the 1970s. Modern homes also account for growing energy use. Between 1970 and 2000 the electricity used for lighting and appliances increased one and a half times.

Up for discussion

What do we use energy for? What would happen if our energy supplies failed? What would be the impact on your home, school, people's workplaces, hospitals and other public services?

The energy gap

Experts warn that, without action, Britain may be generating only 80 per cent of the electricity it needs within the next decade. This shortfall could be disastrous for homes and businesses alike. The gap could be bridged by building new gas or coal-burning power stations to replace those nearing the end of their life. The government is encouraging the development of new technology that will capture emissions of carbon dioxide from these power stations. Building more nuclear power plants is another option that the government is considering, but nuclear energy has many critics. There is also the possibility of developing more renewable power options. Whatever the answers may be, the future of energy in Britain is an issue that urgently needs to be addressed.

THE STATE OF ENERGY TODAY

The first electricity-producing power stations opened in the 1880s. They were powered mainly by coal, oil and petrol. Britain had a plentiful supply of coal, so this was the most common fuel, but gas started to replace coal in the 1990s because it was cheaper and less polluting.

Fossil fuel electricity

Today, nearly three-quarters of Britain's electricity (as opposed to energy) is generated in power stations fuelled by coal, natural gas or oil. These are known as fossil fuels because they are formed from the bodies of animals and plants that died millions of years ago. Coal and oil are burned inside power stations to make steam. This steam moves a spinning electrical generator. Natural gas power stations are set up differently, as the gas spins the electrical generator directly when burned. Gas power stations generate 39 per cent of the electricity used in Britain, while coal generates 34 per cent. Oil accounts for just one per cent.

Air pollution

One of the major drawbacks of coal-fired power stations is that they emit polluting gases. These include sulphur dioxide, which causes acid rain, and nitrogen oxides, which are components of smog.

▲ Sulphur dioxide, produced as a gas from power stations, causes acid rain that can kill trees and erode buildings.

Burning coal also produces carbon dioxide, the main gas behind climate change. In light of this, one-third of Britain's coal power plant capacity is going to close before 2015 in order to follow European Union directives (orders) to cut air pollution, drastically cutting our electricity supplies from this source. While gas power stations are cleaner than coal, they still produce carbon dioxide.

Nuclear power

There are currently 23 nuclear power plants based at nine sites in Britain (the most recent opened in 1995), but they are getting old and need to be shut down. By 2023, only one – Sizewell B in Suffolk – will still be working. The government wants businesses to build new nuclear plants. Ministers believe that without them there will be a big gap in our electricity supply that other options are still far from filling.

Renewable energy

Renewable energy is seen to be key to the future of Britain's energy supply. Abundant and clean, it is hoped that solar, wind, water and other renewables will one day replace fossil fuels as the major energy sources in Britain. Today however, they fill only a small part of our heat and power needs, and have their own drawbacks and limitations (see p.14–21).

▶ A member of Greenpeace protests against the import of polluting coal.

Up for discussion

Electricity provides us with lighting and powers equipment in our homes, offices, factories and schools, but it is only one way in which we use energy. How else do we use energy and what fuels do we use?

DECLINING FOSSIL FUELS

One day, the world's supply of fossil fuels will run out. Estimates vary as to when this will happen, as it depends on a number of factors, including how much energy we use and the availability of other sources of energy. But experts generally agree that we may well witness the disappearance of fossil fuels this century.

Import and export

Britain is producing less and less of its own fossil fuel. We already import more oil than we export. By 2020, three-quarters of the coal we use and 80 per cent of our gas is expected to come from abroad. Britain imports coal from many countries and experts believe there is plenty available, but reserves of oil and natural gas are more limited. The British government recently estimated that global oil reserves will last for another 30 years, though that figure could be doubled through the use of new energy technology. Gas reserves are expected to last for 45 more years, with some experts predicting new reserves to be discovered in the Caspian Sea area in Central Asia. Obtaining this gas and oil from overseas is not necessarily simple though, however great a country's reserves are.

Game of risk

In the first instance, countries have to be willing to sell Britain their gas and oil. In a dispute over prices in 2006, Russia reduced the gas it supplied to the Ukraine via an international pipeline. This had a knock-on effect on other countries as the Ukraine held back some of the gas it planned to pass on to other European nations. The dispute was resolved, but it illustrates how risky obtaining supplies from overseas can be. Pipelines can be damaged by earthquakes or floods, or even targeted by terrorists. There are moves to reduce reliance on pipelines by importing more gas in a liquid form that could then be carried in tankers, like oil.

JUST THE FACTS

- In the 1990s, Britain produced 50 million tonnes of coal a year from 83 deep mines and 122 surface mines. A decade later, we are producing 20 million tonnes of coal a year from 13 deep mines and 31 surface mines.

- In 2005, three-quarters of the coal we used came from abroad, including Australia, Colombia, South Africa and Russia.

- Most of the natural gas used in Britain comes from Norway, Algeria and Qatar.

CASE STUDY
Fossil fuels on the move

Transporting fossil fuels can be difficult and dangerous. In 2006, a pipeline that supplies the former Soviet state of Georgia with gas was damaged by explosions. Gas supplies to Georgia were cut off during the country's coldest winter for 20 years. The Georgian government accused Russia of deliberately damaging the pipeline for political reasons.

Moving fossil fuels by sea can also be hazardous. The oil tanker *Sea Empress* ran aground at Milford Haven in Wales in 1996, spilling its cargo of oil. Local beaches were quickly cleaned up, but it was still more than a year before fish and shellfish caught in the area were considered safe to eat.

▲ September 2006: Workers weld pipes together on the world's longest underwater pipeline between Norway and England. Langeled trunkline is 1,200km long and exports Norwegian gas supplies to Britain. It could eventually supply up to 20 per cent of Britain's gas.

CLIMATE CHANGE

Climate change has been described as the greatest environmental challenge humans have ever faced. The long-term weather patterns of the Earth are believed to be changing because of the accumulation of greenhouse gases in the atmosphere. The main greenhouse gas is carbon dioxide. It is formed in a number of ways, but of greatest concern is the carbon dioxide produced when humans burn fossil fuels.

Carbon build-up

Carbon dioxide acts as a one-way barrier in the atmosphere. It allows energy from the Sun to pass through it to warm the Earth, but only allows some of that heat energy to pass back out into space. Fossil fuels are being burned at such a rate that the carbon dioxide layer in the atmosphere has thickened, trapping too much of this heat.

Rising seas

Global temperatures have already risen. Since records began in 1850, 11 of the past 12 years have been the warmest known. Global warming is causing the seas to heat and expand, and the ice caps and glaciers to melt. Over the last 100 years, sea levels are estimated to have risen by around 17cm and are set to continue to rise. This will have devastating consequences for low-lying countries.

▶ Global warming makes flash floods, like this one in Boscastle, Cornwall, more likely.

The British picture

In Britain, climate change is expected to bring hotter, drier summers and warmer, wetter winters with more torrential rain. The changing climate will extend the growing season for crops, but it could also bring new pests and diseases. Plants, animals and birds from warmer parts of Europe will be seen more often, while native wildlife may move northwards to cooler areas or die out.

Global action

Under the Kyoto Protocol, made in 1997, industrialised countries agreed to cut their greenhouse gas emissions. Some, such as

the USA and Australia, never signed up. India and China did, but were not required to do anything immediately as they were considered developing nations. Not all countries have succeeded in making the greenhouse gas cuts that they promised, although Britain is on course to do so, according to the government. The Kyoto Protocol is now reaching the end of its life. Most countries agree that a new agreement should take its place, but a decision on this has been deferred.

U.S.A 5.43

CANADA 4.88

RUSSIAN FEDERATION 2.85

GERMANY 2.66

JAPAN 2.64

SOUTH KOREA 2.59

UNITED KINGDOM 2.56

ITALY 2.10

CHINA 0.86

INDIA 0.33

◄ Carbon Emissions Greenhouse gases produced (in metric tonnes of carbon) per person per year.

THE NUCLEAR DEBATE

The first British nuclear plant opened in 1956 and nuclear energy quickly became a significant source of energy in Britain, fulfilling almost three per cent of our energy needs. However, despite its role in energy supply and its non-reliance on fossil fuels, for many people nuclear energy's dangers still outweigh its advantages.

For nuclear energy...

Instead of fossil fuels, nuclear plants use uranium, a mineral that is mined and then processed. Inside the nuclear plant, the atoms that make up uranium are split, releasing an explosion of heat. The heat is used to generate electricity. Supporters of nuclear energy argue that its use can help to solve the problems of climate change because carbon dioxide is not produced during the running of the plant, thereby producing 'cleaner' energy.

...And against

Critics of nuclear energy would point out however that carbon dioxide emissions are produced when uranium is mined, transported and stored. Moreover, many people are opposed to nuclear power because the explosion of heat that produces nuclear energy also produces radiation. Radiation is commonly used in X-ray technology and as a cure for some

Dounreay
Torness
Chapel Cross
Calder Hill
Hartlepool
Hunterston
Windscale
Heysham
Wylfa
Trawsfyndd
Sizewell
Bradwell
Oldbury
Berkeley
Hinkley Point
Dungeness
Winfrith

● Decommissioned
● Active

▲ **Location of Electricity-Producing Nuclear Plants in Britain.**

forms of cancer, but exposure to larger amounts can kill. Uranium from power plants continues producing radiation for 1,000 years, and nuclear waste – used nuclear fuel and equipment contaminated with radiation – has to be kept away from living things for all of that time. Currently nearly all of the nuclear waste in Britain is stored at Sellafield in Cumbria. The government plans to build a new underground storage site for old and new nuclear waste, with private companies covering the cost of storing the new waste. A suitable storage site has yet to be chosen, however. On an everyday level, there are also ongoing concerns about the impact of low levels of radiation that are emitted from nuclear sites.

The nuclear future

By 2023, only one nuclear power plant in Britain will still be operating. A report put together by the UK Energy Research Centre in 2005 concluded that their closure will leave a big gap in our electricity supply. The same report advised that the British government should start considering means of building the next phase of nuclear power stations. Faced by the twin threats of energy shortages and climate change, in May 2007, the government published a White Paper. This pledged to triple electricity supply from renewable sources by 2015. However, it also proposed a 'new generation' of nuclear reactors, which will most likely be located on existing sites.

CASE STUDY
The Irish government vs Sellafield

The Sellafield site is run by a company called British Nuclear Group. There are 200 nuclear facilities on the site, some of which are involved in storing nuclear waste. Others process nuclear material. Radioactive water is discharged into the sea that washes the Irish coast just over 90km away. The Irish government argues that this level of radiation is dangerous and went to court in 2001 in an attempt to stop another processing plant operating at the site. The case was unsuccessful, but the Irish government is still urging the European Union to take action.

▼ The site of Sellafield nuclear power plant in Cumbria.

WIND POWER

While fossil fuel supplies dwindle and the debate about nuclear power continues, renewables are fast becoming a popular alternative source of energy. However, there is still much to do to make them available on the scale needed to take the place of more established sources.

Harnessing the wind

Wind power is a leading source of renewable energy, and one that has been successfully adapted to practical use in Britain. There are already enough wind turbines connected to the National Grid to supply one per cent of British power needs – the equivalent demand of one million homes. The energy used in the construction of wind turbines can lead to carbon dioxide being emitted, but once up and running, wind turbines do not create any pollution. Wind is also a free and renewable fuel.

The case against

Large groups of wind turbines divide public opinion. Wind farms are usually built in open countryside where there are no trees or buildings to interfere with the flow of wind passing over the

▼ Wind turbines in the Irish Sea at the North Hoyle offshore wind farm.

turbine, and some people say they spoil the natural landscape. Others worry that birds will be killed by the moving blades or are concerned about noise from the turbines. Setting up wind turbines offshore could get around some of these objections, but offshore wind farms are much more expensive to construct and maintain than onshore ones. The most crucial limitation of wind energy however, is that it produces electricity only when there is wind.

Windy Britain

Britain as an island has the greatest wind resource in Europe. Yet, despite recent investment, it still lags far behind some other European countries, such as Denmark, in terms of converting wind to usable power. Clearly, the future of wind energy is a key issue in the energy debate.

▲ Small turbines that fit on the roof of a house could supply up to 30 per cent of the electricity needs of the average home.

CASE STUDY
The Thames estuary wind farm

In 2006, the British government gave permission to the London Array company to build the world's largest wind farm 20km off the coasts of Kent and Essex. Up to 271 wind turbines will stand above the waves, harnessing enough wind power to meet the electricity needs of 750,000 British homes. The farm will be sited 20km from shore, and it will save around 1.9 million tonnes in carbon emissions a year. The wind farm is supported by green groups, including the Friends of the Earth and the Royal Society for the Protection of Birds, but the Port of London Authority has warned that it may pose a danger to boats.

WATER POWER

The idea of harnessing the power of moving water is not a new one. Water wheels were first developed over 2,000 years ago, and from the middle of the 19th century, the first water turbines came into use. Turbines work by using the movement of falling water to generate a clean, renewable supply of electricity. They are now being used in around 200 hydroelectric plants in Britain. There are two other main types of water-based power – tidal and wave.

Glendoe Hydro Scheme

The largest hydroelectric scheme since the 1960s is at Glendoe in Scotland. It will be fuelled by water flowing downhill into the plant from a new reservoir above Loch Ness. The power station is expected to start generating electricity in 2008, when it will supply enough power to meet the needs of 250,000 British homes. However, there are not many more sites that can be used to generate electricity in this way. Attention has turned to using the flow of rivers and tides to turn turbines instead.

Tidal power

The Stingray pilot project draws energy from the tides as they flow through Yell Sound, off the coast of Shetland in Scotland. The Stingray equipment rests on the seabed, so is under water, but other tidal energy projects are above sea level and create controversy because of the effect they could have on local wildlife habitats. One example of this is the proposed Severn Tidal Barrage. This ambitious project, based around the river Severn estuary in south Wales, could potentially supply around five per cent of Britain's current electricity demand, but work is on hold while its impact on local wildlife sites is assessed.

▶ The Severn Estuary. Supporters of the Severn Tidal Barrage argue that it would generate as much electricity as two to three nuclear power stations.

◀ Waves contain huge amounts of energy, but it is difficult to harness.

▼ Wave power equipment needs to be sturdy to withstand the force of powerful waves.

Wave power

The third type of water energy is wave power. Britain already has the world's first commercially operated wave power plant at Islay, Scotland. This works when waves crash into a chamber in the rocky coastline, forcing the air in the chamber through a turbine that uses the movement to generate electricity. While Islay is only a small plant, it has shown that the difficulties of constructing an electrical generator on a rocky, weather-beaten coastline can be overcome. The company behind the plant, Wavegen, has a bigger scheme planned for the Faroe Islands in the north Atlantic. In the future, Wavegen also plans to build an offshore wave farm near the Orkney Islands, off the north coast of Scotland, which could supply up to 1,400 homes with power.

Making water work

As an island, Britain's water resources are huge. In theory, recoverable wave energy alone could exceed total British demand.

Up for discussion

Do you think the government should proceed with the Severn Barrage, even if it is clear that it would affect wildlife?

If you could choose between electricity from wind or water power, which would you choose and why?

However, it can be difficult to harness and use this energy and, as with wind energy, there are issues involved with making water power environmentally friendly. Out of all of the possible forms of water power, only hydroelectric power is currently widespread and it represents just two per cent of Britain's electrical-generating capacity.

POWER FROM THE SUN

Chemical reactions deep within the Sun's core produce what we know as solar energy, which travels millions of kilometres through space to reach Earth. Such is the power of solar energy that it controls our entire weather system, creating wind and the planet's water cycle. On a sunny day, the Sun beams down the equivalent of 1,000 watts of energy per square metre of the Earth's surface – enough to power all our homes and offices. Solar energy can therefore be another significant source of renewable power, but it needs to be stored effectively.

PV panels

We can capture the Sun's energy with two main types of solar panels. Photovoltaic, or PV, solar panels convert sunlight directly into electricity. PV panels are easy to install and could meet a large portion of British electricity needs. The problem is that although costs are falling, panels are still expensive. A household would currently need to spend between £6,000 and £18,000 to install enough panels to meet most of its energy needs. Panels also generate most energy during the day, making them more suited to schools and businesses than domestic use, although fuel cells (see p.25) may offer a method of storing this energy for night-time demand.

▼ On a sunny day in Britain, the heat given out by the Sun is strong enough to fry an egg on the bonnet of a car!

▲ This solar panel has been designed to heat this home's water, and to provide additional support for the central heating system.

JUST THE FACTS

● All blocks of flats in Barcelona, Spain must have 60 per cent of their hot water supplied through solar water heating.

● For the average British household, solar water-heating panels cost about £3,000–£4,000 to install and save around £50 a year on heating bills.

● Government grants are available to make it cheaper to install solar water-heating and PV panels.

Hot water

The other way of trapping the Sun's power is by using solar water-heating panels alongside a conventional water heater. They concentrate energy from the Sun and use it to heat water. These panels, which are usually installed on the roof, are common in sunny places such as Australia and the countries surrounding the Mediterranean Sea, but they can also work in Britain. In the summer, they can make water hot enough for baths, showers and washing up. In winter, they provide enough heat to take the chill off the water, which means that less electricity or gas is needed to make it hot enough for use.

The future's bright?

Solar energy has a lot of potential as a non-polluting, sustainable energy source, but the main drawback of using it in Britain is the cost. Households would also have to either invest in an expensive battery in which to store the electricity generated during the day to use at night, or buy in extra electricity.

POWER FROM THE EARTH

The Earth itself can provide us with sustainable energy. We can use it to grow plants that can be processed to create fuel for vehicles (biofuel) or burned to make heat or power (biomass). We can also tap into the heat at the centre of the Earth. This is known as geothermal energy.

Biofuels

Certain plants can be processed to extract oil that can be used to fuel a car. The oil is similar to cooking oil and, although it looks very different from the fuel at a petrol station, it does the same job. However, it takes a lot of land to grow crops for fuel. Brazil is close to being energy self-sufficient through investment in plant power. Britain is 35 times smaller than Brazil however, so it is very unlikely that anything like that quantity of energy crops will be grown here. There is also concern that valuable wildlife habitats are being destroyed to grow energy crops, and that there will be an impact on local food supply if farmers switch from growing things to eat to growing biofuel plants.

Plant power

When plants and trees are burned, they release carbon dioxide, the main cause of climate change. But plants and trees also use carbon dioxide to grow, so provided

CASE STUDY
Flower power

Dan Tomlinson (above) from Cambridge has converted his vehicle's engine to run completely on used cooking oil which he collects from kebab vans and turns into fuel for his car at the cost of just 50p a litre. Vehicles that can run on a mixture of plant-based and fossil fuels are already being made by mainstream car manufacturers such as Ford and Saab. In 2006, the first garage pump offering a mix of 85 per cent plant fuel and 15 per cent petrol opened in Norwich.

that enough plants and trees are planted to replace those that have been burned, in theory little extra carbon dioxide is added to the atmosphere in the process. Biomass crops are very useful, as they can be burned to create energy when other sustainable sources, such as wind or solar energy, are in short supply.

Hot Earth

Geothermal energy works by pumping water deep down into the Earth. The water is heated by hot rocks far below the Earth's surface, and returns to the surface in the form of steam. This steam is used to feed turbines that drive huge electrical generators. The steam can also be passed through a heat exchanger to heat houses. There are already a number of geothermal power stations around the world and this form of energy is particularly important in volcanically active countries, such as Iceland and New Zealand. In Britain, there are technological problems to be overcome, but in Cornwall there are promising signs for the future. It is estimated that there is enough energy in the hot granite rocks 6,000m beneath the Earth's surface to supply all of the region's electricity needs in the future.

▼ Young willow trees are harvested to be used as a biomass fuel on a farm in Worcestershire.

Up for discussion

Do you think it is okay to grow crops simply to provide energy? Should crops be kept as a food source?

ENERGY FROM WASTE

Recovering heat and power from burning waste is becoming increasingly widespread in Britain. Incinerators can be designed so that the heat they produce is collected and used to warm local buildings. Incinerators can also be set to generate electricity. However, producing energy from waste is opposed by many environmental pressure groups.

▲ A landfill site in Cardiff, Wales.

Harmful emissions

The main argument against burning waste is the fact that some useful materials, such as paper, plastic and cardboard, are destroyed rather being than recycled or reused. Burning waste also produces carbon dioxide and smoke. Carbon dioxide emissions are well known to be one of the leading causes of climate change and opponents argue that the smoke, despite being cleaned before it is released into the air, still contains harmful chemicals. These chemicals are also concentrated in the ash produced by burning the waste, so this has to be put into a landfill site or tip where it pollutes the environment yet further. The British government considers burning rubbish to be a viable means of generating energy and does not believe the emissions from incinerators to be harmful. In 15 years' time, ministers would like to see 25 per cent of our waste burned to generate electricity, compared with nine per cent now. Work is currently in progress to devise waste collection schemes so that incinerators do not take rubbish that could be recycled.

Methane

As biodegradable waste rots in tips and landfill sites, it produces a greenhouse gas called methane. This gas can have an even more dramatic effect on climate change than carbon dioxide emissions, but it can also be collected and burned to produce heat and electricity. However, to date, not all landfill sites are set up to collect methane. The amount of biodegradable waste allowed to be put in landfill sites is also being reduced in favour of composting, so in time there will be less methane produced.

Farm and forestry waste

Methane gas can also be collected from animal and human sewage. Forestry waste and leftover straw can be also burned to produce energy. Britain has a straw-powered station – currently the world's largest – at Elean, in Cambridgeshire. It generates enough heat and light for 80,000 homes.

JUST THE FACTS

- One tonne of refuse produces 400 cubic metres of gas over 10–20 years.

- The annual total of domestic and industrial waste in Britain could produce as much energy as 20 million tonnes of coal – that's as much energy as we get from British coal mines in one year.

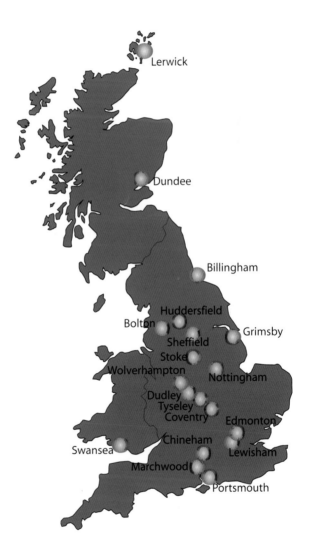

▲ **Landfill Incinerators in Britain**
This map shows the distribution of incinerators in Britain. Though many people see the need for incinerators, few want to live close to one, partly due to the fear of toxic emissions.

INNOVATIONS

People's concern over the future of energy is reflected in exciting innovations that are becoming increasingly popular and widespread. These have been created with the environment and the energy crisis in mind.

Electric motion

Electric vehicles are often in the news and are now becoming more common on the streets. These environmentally-friendly cars do not produce the polluting emissions that standard vehicles do, but they can still have an environmental cost. They run on electric batteries, which rely on regular recharging to keep the vehicle moving. If the battery energy has been produced at a power station that burns fossil fuels, then carbon dioxide will have been emitted at the power station instead. This can of course be avoided by only using electricity from a renewable energy source.

▲ The world's best-selling electric car, the G-Wiz, is cheap to run and completely emission-free.

Gas power

Buses and lorries can have their engines converted to run on natural gas, which is mostly methane, or biogas (see pages 20–21). Natural gas engines are half as noisy as diesel engines and produce less carbon dioxide and pollutants. There are currently about 550 natural gas-powered vehicles in Britain. Most are large trucks, as the gas tanks are currently too big to be compatible with most standard cars.

▲ A London bus is refuelled at Britain's first hydrogen refuelling station in Hornchurch, Essex. In 2005, the government pledged £450,000 to investigate using hydrogen fuel cells to run London buses.

Fuel cells

Fuel cells create electricity and water by combining oxygen and hydrogen. The first fuel-celled vehicles are already in use, and fuel cells will also be important in the future of renewable energy. When wind- and solar-powered generators are producing electricity, fuel cells can work in reverse, converting the electricity to oxygen and hydrogen. The hydrogen can then be stored for conversion back to water and electricity when needed.

New technology

New energy technology is one area that the British government is committed to exploring, particularly if, as with hydrogen fuel cells, it makes renewable sources of energy more practical. Carbon sequestration is one area of technology that could allow renewables more time to become established. This involves capturing the carbon dioxide produced when coal and gas are burned and storing it in empty oil fields, so that it doesn't reach the atmosphere. If we learn how to do this on a large scale, it could be argued that coal, which is more plentiful than oil or gas, could be burned to generate energy without creating further climate change. This technology however, like many alternative energy sources, is still very new.

JUST THE FACTS

● Sweden has the largest fleet of biogas-powered cars in the world – 7,000 vehicles.

● Electric cars can park and charge up for free in some London car parks.

SAVING ENERGY

Britain is facing a huge gap between its energy demand and the energy available for use. The pressure to find new sources of clean energy can be eased by reducing the amount of electricity and fuels that we use.

Global demand

Between 2003 and 2005, household gas bills went up by 38 per cent and electricity bills went up by 30 per cent. Shops, offices, hospitals, factories and schools have all seen their bills soar, too. The reasons for this are complex, but prices will continue to increase as huge, developing countries such as China and India need more energy to advance their industries and improve the living standards of their people.

The other reason for our increasing gas bills is that Britain currently imports gas from just a few countries, thereby restricting our chance of finding a cheaper price. To give us greater choice, a new gas supply route is being built – the Langeled pipeline from Norway (see page 9). Gas suppliers are also investing in facilities to import gas in tankers in a liquid form – Liquified Natural Gas or LNG. This will give us a greater choice of suppliers. In 2007, Britain had only two ports that could handle this type of cargo – the Isle of Grain in Kent and Teesside GasPort.

◀ Solar panels can help households to reduce energy use.

Energy economy

We can cut energy use by 30 per cent simply by changing our behaviour and investing in tried and tested measures, such as improving the insulation of our homes, using low-energy light bulbs and setting washing machines to wash at lower temperatures. The British government is trying to persuade people to save energy through publicity campaigns and by offering grants to people on low incomes, but the biggest incentive for householders and businesses to save energy will probably come from the rising cost of energy itself.

Carbon cost

One way to reduce the amount of carbon dioxide generated by the increased demand for energy is to put a price on carbon. The European Union has done this for major generators of carbon dioxide through its emissions trading scheme. This gives individual businesses a set amount of carbon that they are allowed to produce. If they need more, they have to buy allowances from other carbon dioxide producers who have allowances to spare. It has also been suggested that individuals should have a carbon allowance too. If they decided they wanted to commute to work by car, take long flights or perform other activities that produce high amounts of carbon, they would then have to save energy in other areas of their life.

JUST THE FACTS

Here are some energy-saving suggestions:

● Unplug equipment such as laptops and mobile phones once they are fully charged, otherwise they will keep drawing electricity.

● TVs, videos, stereos and computers left on standby can use 40–70 per cent of the energy they use when they are switched on.

● Try to boil only enough water for your needs to avoid wasting energy.

CASE STUDY
The ExCeL carbon challenge

The London International Exhibition Centre (ExCeL) is the largest open exhibition space in northern Europe. It used to have a massive energy bill – £1.1 million a year – mostly spent on lighting and air conditioning.

It asked the Carbon Trust, which offers businesses advice on saving energy to help it cut its costs. Through a better understanding of how to use equipment efficiently and by making staff aware of the need to save energy, the centre cut its yearly bill by a third and greatly reduced carbon emissions.

▼ ExCeL is over 90,000 square metres in size and holds up to 20,000 visitors.

GOVERNMENT AND CITIZEN ACTION

Nearly all of the energy used in Britain is produced by private companies that choose to invest in the energy sources that will make them the most profit. However, national and local governments and even individuals can play a part in directing the future of energy in Britain.

Government pressure

Private companies are responsible for looking into new means of generating or importing electricity. However, the government can steer companies towards certain sources by paying for research into alternative energies and through policies, taxes and grants. This gives financial support to new renewable energy projects.

▼ Energy in Britain is at a crossroads. The decisions the government makes now will have a great impact on the future.

New nuclear

Renewable sources still meet just four per cent of Britain's energy needs. The government wants to see this rise to ten per cent by 2010 and 20 per cent by 2020. Nevertheless, ministers are convinced that we need new nuclear power stations to bridge the gap left by the closure of ageing fossil fuel plants and nuclear power stations. The government also argues that investing in nuclear power will make us

less reliant on imported fuels and will help us to reduce Britain's carbon emissions. To encourage businesses to build new plants, the government is looking at changing the planning system to make it easier for building projects of national significance, such as nuclear power stations, to obtain planning permission. At present, they can be held up for years by pressure groups or by the supporters of rival schemes.

Government and the public

The government consults the public on changes to a number of policies, and this is one way for individuals to get involved in influencing the future of energy in Britain. In 2006, the government opened a public debate on the controversial issue of creating new nuclear power stations.

Citizen action

As well as saving energy where possible, people can play a part in the energy debate by choosing where their heat and power comes from. They can decide to buy from companies such as Good Energy or Ecotricity that supply renewably generated power. Individuals may even choose to make their own energy by installing wind turbines or solar panels at home.

CASE STUDY
Saving energy in Woking

The town of Woking in Surrey is renowned for its work on renewable fuels and energy efficiency. The town's council has reduced its energy consumption by 40 per cent in nine years. It has a range of PV panels and its own local electrical grid system that reduces energy leakages. It also has the only fuel cell Combined Heat and Power plant in Britain,

▶ The swimming pool at Woking's solar- and fuel cell-powered leisure centre.

which is linked to the town's swimming pool and sheltered housing. As a result, the town centre is completely

self-sufficient for electricity. Better still, electricity is 1p a unit cheaper than from the National Grid.

ELIN	
Z752533	
PETERS	27-Feb-2012
333.79	£12.99

GLOSSARY

Acid rain Rain formed when industrial emissions combine with water in the atmosphere.

Atmosphere The thick layer of gases that surround the Earth.

Atom A tiny particle of matter.

Biodegradable Able to rot away.

Biofuel Fuels made from plants, which are used to power cars.

Biomass Plant materials or animal waste burned to generate energy. Biomass fuels are usually solid, while biofuels are usually liquid.

Carbon dioxide A gas present in air that is thought to be the main cause of climate change.

Carbon sequestration Capturing carbon dioxide and storing it so that it doesn't escape into the atmosphere.

Climate change Long-term changes to the world's weather patterns.

Combined Heat and Power Plant A power plant where excess heat is piped off and used to heat nearby buildings.

Compost Decayed organic matter that can be used as a fertiliser.

Emissions Substances that are given off into the air, such as vehicle exhaust fumes.

Energy Heat and power.

Environmentalists People concerned about protecting the environment.

Export To sell goods or services to foreign countries.

Fossil fuels Oil, natural gas and coal. They are known as fossil fuels because they were formed from the remains of living things over the course of millions of years.

Fuel cell A device in which chemicals react to generate electricity.

Generator A machine that converts energy into electricity.

Hydroelectric Electricity generated by water from a dam or river flowing through a set of turbines.

Incinerators A place where material, usually waste, is burned.

Kyoto Protocol A agreement made by industrialised countries to reduce greenhouse gas emissions. As of December 2006, 169 countries had joined the agreement.

Import To buy in goods or services from foreign countries.

Insulation Protective layers of material that prevent heat from escaping.

Oxygen A gas present in air. It can be combined with hydrogen in a fuel cell to make electricity.

Photovoltaic Generating electricity from sunlight.

Renewable energy A source of energy that does not run out and is constantly renewed, such as wind or solar power.

Smog A type of air pollution formed when sunlight reacts with emissions, particularly vehicle exhaust fumes, in the atmosphere.

Sustainable Capable of being used sustainably; that is to meet our present needs without preventing future generations from meeting theirs.

Toxic Harmful.

Turbine A machine in which moving gases or liquids cause a set of blades to rotate. This rotation can generate electricity.

White Paper A document that sets out the government's intended action on an area of concern, for example energy.

FURTHER INFO

The Energy Debate: The Pros and Cons of Coal, Gas, and Oil by Sally Morgan (Hodder Wayland, 2007)

Sustainable Futures: Energy by John Stringer (Evans Brothers, 2006)

The Energy Debate: Biomass Power by Isobel Thomas (Hodder Wayland, 2007)

Your Environment: Future Energy by Sally Morgan (Franklin Watts, 2005)

WEBSITES

www.bnfl.com
The website for British Nuclear Fuels, a group of companies that generates nuclear electricity and deals with radioactive waste.

www.carbontrust.co.uk
A government-funded agency that helps businesses deal with climate change.

www.defra.gov.uk
The website of the UK government department responsible for waste policy in England – the Department for Environment, Food and Rural Affairs.

www.detni.gov.uk
The website of the Northern Ireland Department of Enterprise, Trade and Investment, which carries energy policy for Northern Ireland.

www.dti.gov.uk
The website of the UK government department responsible for energy policy – the Department of Trade and Industry.

www.ehsni.gov.uk
The website of the Environment and Heritage Service, which carries the waste policy for Northern Ireland.

www.energy-retail.org.uk
A trade association of energy retailers.

www.energysavingtrust.org.uk
The Energy Saving Trust, a government-funded organisation promoting energy efficiency and renewable energy generation.

www.foe.co.uk
The website of the environmental campaigning group Friends of the Earth.

www.fuel-cell-bus-club.com
The website for European pilot projects for fuel cell-powered vehicles.

www.greenpeace.org.uk
The website of Greenpeace, an environmental campaigning group.

www.northernireland.gov.uk
The website of the Northern Ireland Executive.

www.scotland.gov.uk
The website of the Scottish Executive, which is responsible for national waste policy and some aspects of energy policy in Scotland.

www.wales.gov.uk
The portal website to the Welsh Assembly Government, which is responsible for national waste policy and some aspects of energy policy in Wales.

Note to parents and teachers: Every effort has been made by the Publishers to ensure that these websites are suitable for children, that they are of the highest educational value, and that they contain no inappropriate or offensive material. However, because of the nature of the Internet, it is impossible to guarantee that the contents of these sites will not be altered. We strongly advise that Internet access is supervised by a responsible adult.

INDEX

These are the lists of contents for each title in *British Issues:*

Future Energy
The importance of energy • The state of energy today • Declining fossil fuels • Climate change • The nuclear debate • Wind power • Water power • Power from the Sun • Power from the Earth • Energy from waste • Innovations • Saving energy • Government and citizen action

Population Change
Britain's changing faces • Measuring change • People in the past • Population at work • Changing families • New lifestyles • Life moves • Trading places • Immigrants and emigrants • The European Union • Cultural identity • Ageing population • Looking to the future

Sporting Success
2012 • A rich history • Governing bodies •Funding • Facilities • Sport and society • The business of sport • Success stories • Sport and education • Fair play • Sport and the media • Sport and national pride • Looking towards 2012

Sustainable Cities
What does it mean to be a sustainable city? • Urban versus rural populations • Planning sustainable cities • Urban regeneration • Issues in the south-east • Stuck in the city • City movers • Sustainable energy • Water • Dealing with waste • Urban wildlife • Cities of opportunity • Vision of the future

Waste and Recycling
What is waste? • Throwaway society • What happens to waste? • Why waste matters • Managing waste • Reduce and reuse • Recycle! • How recycling happens • Composting • Energy from waste • Why don't we recycle more? • Changing the rules • A way to go

Water
Desert Britain? • The water industry • Water supply • Household water • Industry and agriculture • A growing gap • Climate change • The cost of water • Saving water • Drinking water • Water and the environment • Planning for the future • New technology